Building Jewish Iden

OUR COMMUNITY

By Judy Dick

BEHRMAN HOUSE
www.behrmanhouse.com

Design: Terry Taylor Studio
Project manager: Dena Neusner

Copyright © 2012 Behrman House, Inc.
Published by Behrman House, Inc.
Springfield, NJ 07081
www.behrmanhouse.com

ISBN: 978-0-87441-861-3
Printed in the United States of America

The publisher gratefully acknowledges the following sources of photographs and graphic images:
(T=top, B=bottom, L=left, R=right)
Art Resource/Erich Lessing 16T; Behrman House 34B; Dreamstime: Blueenayim 25T; Mary Francell-Sharfstein 4R, 44; Israel Ministry of Tourism 27B; iStockphoto: kristian sekulic cover, 1, 2-3, pederk 36B, Tova Teitelbaum 39, Ryan Howe 40B; Alberto Jona Falco 5L, 33; Terry Kaye 10T, 28; Chavie Knapp 4L, 9; Lenny Krayzelburg 5R; Mazi Melesa 18B; Elisa Pener 8B; Shutterstock: Odelia Cohen (cover pendant), Lisa F. Young (cover challah), Asaf Eliason (cover Shalom art), Mikhail Levit (cover goblet), AISPIX by Image Source (cover Torah scroll), Helga Esteb (Spielberg) 5B, Malgorzata Kistryn 6-7, Djordje Radivojevic 8L, Margot Petrowski 13T, Valentyn Volkov 13BL, 13BR Rey Kamensky, wandee007 14L, badahos 14R, Zurijeta 15, Luba 16B, MANDY GODBEHEAR 17, CLM 18T, Pakhnyushcha 18-19 background, Christopher Parypa 19, Antenna International, 20-21 background, Kobby Dagan 20B, Stephen Mcsweeny 22T, Picsfive 22-23 chain, Alexander Kaludov 24, Arkady Mazor 25BL, Gregory Gerber 25B R and middle, Eric Isselée 26B, M.Unal Ozmen 27T, trubach 30L, Keith Levit 30R, Mordechai Meiri 31, 32 shofar, Carmen Medlin 31 dove, Phish Photography 31 tablets, AISPIX by Image Source 31 Torah crown, pokku 31 menorah carving, Howard Sandler 31 chai necklace, pavelr 31 hamantaschen, Olaf Speier 31 latkes, AlexGul 31 matzah, Ledo 31 horseradish, Johan Swanepoel 31 apple, clearimages 31 challah, Mordechai Meiri 32 gragger, Mikhail Levit 32 Kiddush cup, Mordechai Meiri 32 menorah, Alexander Gordeyev 32 candlestick, CLM 32 dreidel, MG Photos 32 seder plate, billdayone 32 cabinet, AISPIX by Image Source 34T, untung 35, Sailorr 38, Wildstyle 38B, Golden Pixels LLC 40T, Morgan Lane Photography 42, Tropinina Olga 43, mangostock 44T, Dmitriy Shironosov 45T, Aptyp_koK 45B, CREATISTA 46; Arthur Szyk Society www.szyk.org 22BL; Wikimedia Commons: 4B, Smallbones 10B, 23L, 23 middle (painting by Thomas Sully), 23R, 26T, 48; The Max Stern Collection, Yeshiva University Museum 36T.

The publisher wishes to acknowledge the following sources for quotes:
Ginsburg, page 4: courtesy of BabagaNewz.
Krayzelburg, page 5: courtesy of BabagaNewz.
Spielberg, page 5: Frank Sanello. *Spielberg: The Man, the Movies, the Mythology*. Taylor Publishing Company, 1996
Messinger, page 43: Judea and Ruth Pearl, ed. *I Am Jewish*. Jewish Lights, 2004

Library of Congress Cataloging-in-Publication Data
Dick, Judy.
 Our community / by Judy Dick.
    p. cm. -- (Building Jewish identity ; v. 1)
 ISBN 978-0-87441-861-3
 1. Judaism--Juvenile literature. I. Title.
 BM573.D525 2012
 296--dc23
                    2012006281

Dedicated to my wonderful Grandma,
who gave me my lifelong love of books.

– Judy Dick

CONTENTS

CHAPTER 1

JEWISH LIKE ME

What does being Jewish mean to you? What do you have in common with Jewish actors, judges, athletes, scientists, teachers, and students? The Jewish community is made up of all kinds of people, all over the world—including you.

I really like cooking for Shabbat with my family. We make chocolate chip cookies and brownies every week.

—Amalya;
Teaneck, New Jersey

For my bar mitzvah project, I collected mosquito nets for Jewish children in Ethiopia. These nets help protect families from malaria. For every net we sent to Ethiopia, we saved somebody's life.

—Jack;
Alpharetta, Georgia

I was born and raised as a Jew, and I'm proud of it. The demand for justice runs through the entirety of the Jewish tradition. I hope... I will have the strength and the courage to remain constant in the service of that demand.

—Ruth Bader Ginsburg,
United States Supreme Court Justice

Being Jewish

Being Jewish means something different for each of us. Your Jewish identity is shaped by your family, your community, and the things that you do every day. Your Jewish values affect the way you look at the world and make decisions about your life. Being Jewish affects the foods you eat, the holidays you celebrate, and the stories you learn.

My favorite story from the Torah is the creation of the world: light and darkness, land and water, animals and birds. But the best of all is the invention of Shabbat.

—Joseph; Milan, Italy

I'm involved with a ...student athlete exchange program that teaches American and Israeli high school athletes how to become better citizens using values taught in sports.

—Lenny Krayzelburg, Olympic gold medalist in swimming

When my son was born...I decided I wanted my kids raised Jewish, as I was ...[and] to be proud of the fact that they were members of the oldest tribe in history.

—Steven Spielberg, movie director and producer

Jewish Me

There are many sides to the "Jewish You." Your family history, the way you celebrate Jewish holidays, and your Hebrew name are all parts of your Jewish identity.

Create an image board that illustrates the "Jewish You." Complete the items on the board and add more items that reflect your Jewish life.

My Hebrew name is:

_____

Draw a picture or attach a photo of yourself or your family at a Jewish event.

Add the Jewish activities that you do each week to your calendar.

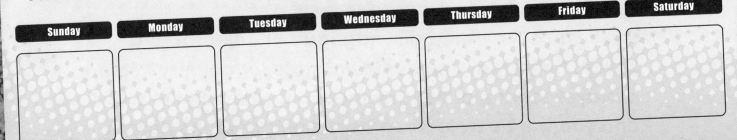

Sunday	Monday	Tuesday	Wednesday	Thursday	Friday	Saturday

Draw your favorite Jewish object
and write a caption for the picture.

List three questions that you have about being Jewish.
Talk about them with your friends or family.

_____

_____

_____

7

CHAPTER 2

PIECES OF THE PUZZLE: Jewish Community

Have you ever visited a synagogue or celebrated a Jewish holiday in another town, state, or country? Join a prayer service or holiday meal anywhere in the world and you will be welcomed as a member of the Jewish community.

A Global Jewish Family

You are part of a very large Jewish family. You are connected to other Jews in your town, across the country, and around the world. You are a piece of a very complex puzzle. When you put all the pieces together, they create a picture of our whole Jewish community: people who may look and dress differently from each other and speak different languages in their daily lives, but who share a history, the Torah, Jewish values, the Hebrew language, and many holiday traditions.

Close-Up on Community

A community is a group of people who have something in common with each other. You belong to many communities—your family, your school, your neighborhood, perhaps a musical group or sports team. List some communities that you belong to here.

Name of Community	Some things we have in common
My family	We're related. We live together. We love each other.

Meet Amalya

Prize-winning gymnast Amalya balances her busy schedule with a commitment to Jewish community and Torah study.

First Competition: It was right before my cousin's bat mitzvah. I didn't even know that I came in first place because I had to rush out early—my mother found out and told me later at the bat mitzvah!

Jewish Community: I go to a Jewish school and a Jewish sports camp. I also am part of a ḥavurah, a Torah study group in my neighborhood that meets every Shabbat.

Message: Learning new skills for gymnastics is challenging. It's also hard when I miss some gymnastic events that take place on Jewish holidays. But being Jewish is important to me, so it's worth it!

Synagogue Central

In biblical times, the **Temple** in Jerusalem, in the Land of Israel, was the center for Jewish worship. Jews came from far and wide to bring sacrifices and celebrate major holidays together. Originally built by King Solomon around three thousand years ago, the Temple stood for centuries until it was destroyed by invaders. It was followed by the Second Temple, which stood until the year 70 CE.

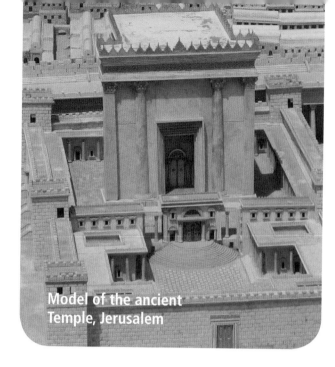
Model of the ancient Temple, Jerusalem

But as Jews settled in many places around the world, they no longer had one central Temple for all the people. Instead, Jews in each community came together at the local synagogue to pray, study the Torah, celebrate, and help each other. In some communities today, the synagogue may be called a temple or shul. Jews today also gather in Jewish community centers for cultural events, learning, socializing, athletics, and more. Do you do any of these activities at your synagogue, temple, shul, or community center?

Synagogue designed by Frank Lloyd Wright, Elkins Park, Pennsylvania

Inside the Synagogue

At the heart of the synagogue are the people within its walls. Many people help to build Jewish life in the community and to make everything run smoothly.

Complete this set of cards for the people you may meet at your synagogue. Then attach a drawing or photograph. Who else adds to the Jewish life in your community?

Meet the Rabbi

Name: Rabbi _____

We often find the rabbi here:

_____

We can count on the rabbi to…

_____

Some important things the rabbi does:

_____

and _____

and _____

Meet the Cantor

Name: Cantor _____

We often find the cantor here:

_____

We can count on the cantor to…

_____

Some important things the cantor does:

_____

and _____

and _____

Meet the Morah or Moreh

Name: _____

We often find the morah/moreh here:

_____

We can count on the morah/moreh to…

_____

Some important things the morah/moreh does:

_____

and _____

and _____

Meet a Student

Name: _____

We often find this student here:

_____

We can count on this student to…

_____

Some important things this student does:

_____

and _____

and _____

A Community Without Borders

The Jewish community is bigger than your family, your school, or your synagogue. We share common experiences and backgrounds with Jewish people around the world. We call this worldwide Jewish community **Am Yisrael**, which means "the people of Israel."

As part of Am Yisrael, we share much of our history and stories, we observe the same or similar holiday rituals, we study and pray in the same language, Hebrew, and we share uniquely Jewish values.

Building Blocks of Jewish Identity

Help build Jewish identity by filling in examples of the things we have in common with other members of Am Yisrael. One example has been filled in for you.

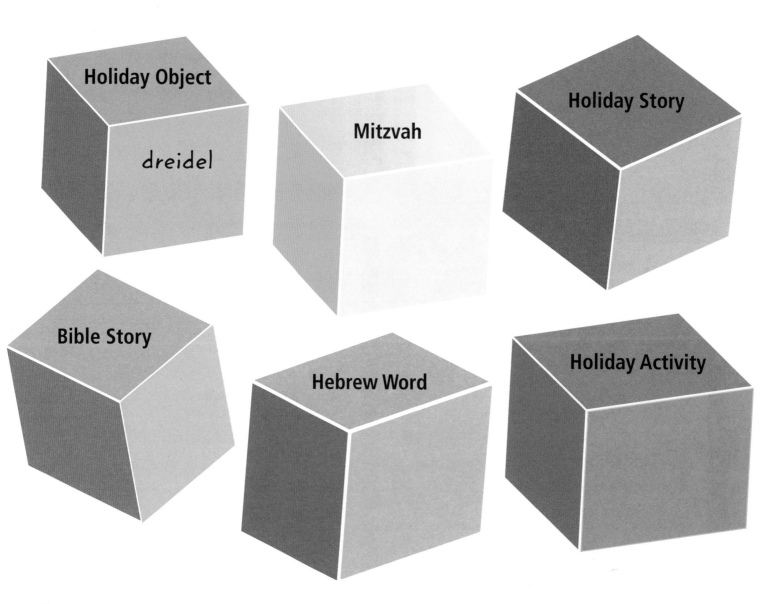

Holiday Object — dreidel

Mitzvah

Holiday Story

Bible Story

Hebrew Word

Holiday Activity

Jewish Diversity

Does this mean the people in Am Yisrael are all the same? Not a chance. In the United States and Canada, a Jewish family might belong to a Reform, Conservative, Reconstructionist, or Orthodox synagogue. These groups approach some Jewish laws and practices in different ways.

Most Jews in America are Ashkenazi. That means their ancestors originally came from European countries such as Germany and Poland. Other Jews are Sephardi, with ancestors from Mediterranean countries such as Spain. These two groups have some different customs, such as different recipes for the ḥaroset we eat during the Passover seder.

And Jews may be white, black, or brown; we may come from single-parent families, blended families, or other nontraditional families; and we may be Jews by birth or by choice.

There's plenty of diversity within the Jewish community, yet we all share a common identity and commitment to Judaism.

Talk about It

The great Jewish teacher Hillel said, "Do not separate yourself from the community" (Pirkei Avot 2:5). In what ways are you involved in the Jewish community? What do you like about being part of a community?

Your Turn

Which is your favorite? Have a taste test!

Ashkenazi ḥaroset: Chunky mix of apples, walnuts, sweet red wine or grape juice, cinnamon, sugar.

Sephardi ḥaroset: Smooth mixture of dates, bananas, raisins, honey, cinnamon, allspice, ginger, nutmeg.

Find complete recipes at www.behrmanhouse.com/passover.

CHAPTER 3

A RICH HERITAGE: History and Stories

What are your favorite kinds of stories? Action and adventure? Fantasy? History? Legends? Jewish stories come in all of these types and help define who we are as individuals and as part of the Jewish community.

The Power of a Story

A classic Jewish folktale tells of a king who owned a beautiful and rare diamond. The king was upset one day to discover a scratch on its clear surface. No one could fix it. Then one young diamond cutter found a solution. He carved a beautiful rose in the diamond, using the scratch as the stem, and so turned the imperfection into a work of art. The king was overjoyed with the stone, which was now even more precious. From this we learn that we all have the ability to turn our weaknesses into strengths.

Stories: A Shared Treasury

Through stories we share our history and experiences, we connect to our past and prepare for the future, and like the story of the rose in the diamond, we teach important lessons. Our oldest stories come from the Bible, which we call the *Tanach* in Hebrew. The first part of the Tanach is the **Torah**, which contains our most important stories and laws.

Stories from the Tanach have been retold countless times. They have inspired commentaries, folktales, legends, art, music, and movies from generations of rabbis, teachers, storytellers, writers, and artists.

Tanach Jeopardy

Word Bank: Miriam, shepherd, Adam, Egypt, Eve

How many of these stories from the Tanach do you know? Fill in questions for each answer.

1. The Torah begins with the story of Creation and *these* two people, the first man and woman.

   Who are _____ and _____ ?

2. Joseph, famous for wearing a special coat, was sold into slavery in *this* country.

   What is _____ ?

3. *This* famous sister helped her brother Moses lead the Exodus.

   Who is _____ ?

4. A brave soldier and talented musician, King David had *this* job as a young boy.

   What is _____ ?

A Jewish Library

The Jewish library doesn't end with the Bible. Match the Jewish stories to the descriptions.

1. Stories about a Jewish boy no bigger than a thumb.

2. A town in classic Jewish folktales where the people are as foolish as can be.

3. A wildly famous children's book by Jewish author/illustrator Maurice Sendak.

4. A famous comic book hero created by a Jewish writer and illustrator team.

   a. Chelm (*The Wise Men of Chelm*)

   b. *Superman* (comic book by Jerry Siegel and Joe Shuster)

   c. *The Adventures of K'ton Ton* (by Sadie Rose Weilerstein)

   d. *Where the Wild Things Are*

What is your favorite Jewish story?

_____

_____

Answers: 1c, 2a, 3d, 4b

In the Beginning

Where does our community's story begin? The Bible introduces us to a man named Abraham, the first Jew. Most people at the time of Abraham worshipped idols, statues they believed were gods. According to Jewish tradition, Abraham's own father, Terach, made and sold idols. But Abraham stood up for his belief in one God, even risking his father's anger for his beliefs.

Jewish tradition tells the story of how, while Terach was away on a trip, Abraham took a stick and smashed all the idols, except for the largest one. He put the stick in this idol's hand. When his father returned and angrily asked who had destroyed the idols, Abraham explained that the biggest idol got into a fight with the smaller ones and killed them. "You know that's impossible!" said Abraham's father. "Of course it's impossible," Abraham replied. Abraham had made his point that idols did not have any power.

Canaanite idol

Turning to the Torah

The Torah tells us how Abraham and his wife Sarah, at God's command, left their home in ancient Iraq and traveled to the land of Canaan, which is now Israel. God then made a covenant, an agreement or promise, with Abraham.

> Here is My Covenant with you. You shall be the father of many nations. . . . I will establish My Covenant between Me and you and your descendants . . . to be your God. . . . And I will give to you and your descendants . . . the whole land of Canaan, as an eternal inheritance. . . . And you must keep My Covenant—you and your descendants throughout the generations.
>
> (Genesis 17:4, 17:7–9)

What does God promise to Abraham? _____

What does God expect in return? _____

A Brit Come True

Many years after Abraham and Sarah settled in Canaan, a famine forced their grandson Jacob, also known as Israel, to move south to Egypt with his family. Jacob's family was called the people of Israel, or **Israelites**. Generations later, a new pharaoh came to power in Egypt and made the Israelites slaves.

But the story wasn't over for the Israelites. Instead, the Torah tells us, God chose the great leader Moses to lead the Israelite slaves from Egypt to freedom. On their way back to Canaan through the desert, the Jewish people renewed their commitment to the original covenant made between God and Abraham, when they received a precious gift from God at Mount Sinai—the Torah. A new chapter in the life of the Jewish nation had begun.

The Torah has been handed down for thousands of years, from Moses to each of us.

Why do you think the Torah has remained so important to us for so many years?

Words to Know: Brit

The Hebrew word for covenant or agreement is *brit*. Write your own explanation for the word *brit*. Describe a time in your life when you made an agreement with someone. Why was it important for both of you to keep the agreement?

Holiday Stories

Many Jewish holidays are designed to help us remember the stories of our people.

- On Passover, we retell the story of the Israelites' Exodus from Egypt, setting them on the path toward the Land of Israel.

- On Ḥanukkah, we recount the Maccabees' victory in ancient Israel over the Greeks and the miracle of the oil that lasted for eight days.

- On Purim, we read the story of Esther and drown out the name of Haman, who plotted to destroy the Jewish people.

How have our people kept these stories alive for so many generations? In addition to reading or telling the stories on each of these holidays, we use various objects, and even foods, to help us remember the details.

Adding New Chapters

The story of Am Yisrael continues today. Each generation adds to our community's history. Some Jewish families have even experienced their own miraculous exodus. Mazi, an Ethiopian-Israeli Jew, remembers the eventful day, May 24, 1991, when she and her family escaped from war-torn Ethiopia, a country in Africa.

In a secret mission called Operation Solomon, more than fourteen thousand Jews were airlifted from Ethiopia to Israel on forty-one flights in just thirty-six hours. Mazi, who was twelve years old, recalls how her life changed in a short time:

We each received a sticker with a number that we put on our foreheads, and we got on a bus to the airport. We were so happy! We held each other's hands as we boarded a huge jumbo jet. We had never been on a plane before. We all sat on the floor—the seats had been taken out to squeeze in as many families as possible. About four hours later, we saw Israel from afar

Holiday Mad Libs

Choose a verb and a noun for each of the holidays below. Then fill in the blanks to tell how each object or food helps you remember the holiday story.

1. On Ḥanukkah, I _____ the _____ . This helps me remember that _____
     (verb)   (noun)

_____ .

2. On Purim, I _____ the _____ . This reminds me that _____
     (verb)   (noun)

_____ .

3. During Passover, I _____ the _____ . This is because _____
      (verb)   (noun)

_____ .

Word Bank: verbs

light	cook
eat	taste
play with	hear
shake	spin
read	

Word Bank: nouns

Ḥanukkah candles	latkes
ḥaroset	maror (bitter herbs)
dreidel	matzah
gragger (noisemaker)	Megillah
haggadah	sufganiyot (jelly donuts)
hamantashen	

---

for the first time ever. People were so grateful when we landed in Israel that they kissed the ground. I kissed the ground, too. Then Israeli soldiers came to show us to our new homes in Israel. It was all so quick! At our seders today my father says that just as the biblical Exodus came true for the ancient Israelites, so, too, the Ethiopian Jews finally had their Exodus. Our dream had come true!

Your Turn

Ask your parents or grandparents to tell you some family stories from long ago. If possible, record their words on paper or video. What family stories will you tell your children and grandchildren some day? How do stories—whether they're Bible stories, Jewish folktales, or family stories—connect us with Am Yisrael, the Jewish people?

Tracing Your Roots

Today, the United States has one of the largest Jewish communities in the world. If Jewish history began in the Land of Israel, why are there now Jews living in North America? Or Europe, South America, and Australia?

After the Exodus from Egypt, the Israelites spent forty years in the desert and then settled in Canaan, later known as Israel. King David made Jerusalem the capital of Israel, and Jewish life flourished in Israel for hundreds of years.

But invading armies changed our history. After the Babylonians and, later, the Romans conquered ancient Israel, many Jews were uprooted from their homes and had to build a new life in exile, far away from their homeland. And so it was that Jews built vibrant new communities all around the world. We refer to living outside of Israel as living in the **Diaspora**.

NORTH AMERICA

Canada

United States

Brazil

Argentina

My Heart Is in the East

For almost two thousand years, Jews in the Diaspora dreamed of returning to Israel and to Jerusalem. In 1948, the modern country of Israel was founded, and today Jerusalem is once again the capital of a Jewish state. Jews come from around the world to pray at Israel's holiest site, the **Kotel**. Also called the Western Wall, the Kotel is nearly all that remains of the ancient Temple complex.

Find Israel on the map. When Jews pray, we face in the direction of Jerusalem, which means Jews in North America face east. How does facing Jerusalem when we pray make us feel connected to Israel and to Jews around the world?

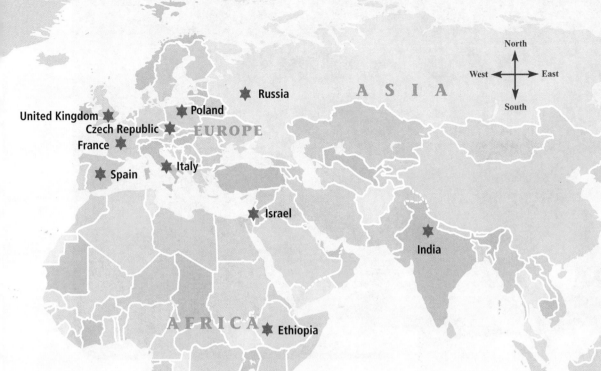

Identifying Diaspora Communities

Unscramble the words to find the names of some countries where Jews went to live. These countries and more are marked on the map.

Did You Know . . .

_____ NSIPA The king and queen forced all the Jews to leave in 1492.

_____ DNOPLA Jews built beautiful wooden synagogues here.

_____ AITEHOIP Jews were airlifted from this country's capital to Israel in 1991.

_____ AIDNI Jews were living in this country as early as the eighth century CE.

_____ _____ CCZHE LREPBUCI The oldest synagogue still in use stands here, in Prague.

_____ LATIY The first printed Hebrew Bible was published here, in 1488.

_____ CAFERN Jews here were the first in Europe to receive equal rights, during the nineteenth century.

_____ _____ EDITUN TTEASS The Jewish community here began with just twenty-three Jewish immigrants, but now totals about six-and-a-half million.

_____ ADACNA Jewish citizens here speak French and English, the country's two official languages.

Links in the Chain of Tradition

Each generation of Am Yisrael passes on Jewish tradition to the next. This means that we are each a link in a chain that stretches throughout history. From the Land of Israel to Babylonia to Spain, Jewish rabbis and teachers studied the Torah. They wrote important books of commentary that help us understand the Torah, and define many of the Jewish practices we observe today.

Meet some great Jewish teachers from across the centuries:

HILLEL
(first century BCE):
"Be one who loves peace, who loves all people, and who brings them closer to Torah." (Pirkei Avot 1:12)

JUDAH HANASI
(second century CE):
"I have learned much from my teachers, and even more from my friends. But I have learned the most from my students."
(Talmud, Makkot 6a)

How Will You Continue the Chain?

We can all be part of the chain, by first being students of the Torah and then its teachers.

If you could ask one of these great teachers a question, what would it be?

_____

Hundreds of years from now, what would you like people to remember about you?

_____

Talk about It

How does learning about your history connect you to Jews around the world?

SOLOMON SCHECHTER (1847–1915):
My discovery of a treasury of medieval Jewish books and letters in an old synagogue in Cairo shed light on an important time in Jewish history.

MAIMONIDES
(1135–1204):
I answered religious questions from Jews around the world while serving as physician to the sultan of Egypt.

REBECCA GRATZ
(1781–1869):
I started one of the earliest Jewish Sunday schools in America, in 1838.

NECHAMA LEIBOWITZ
(1905–1997):
I taught Torah to thousands of students and received the Israel Prize in education in 1956.

CHAPTER 4

SPEAKING THE SAME LANGUAGE: Hebrew

In how many languages can you say hello? With the Hebrew word שָׁלוֹם shalom, Jews all around the world can say "hello" to each other (and "good-bye" and "peace"). We share this unique language, Hebrew, with the whole Jewish community.

The Importance of a Common Language

The Bible tells the story of the Tower of Babel, about people who came together to build a city with a tower that would reach heaven. They made bricks and started building higher and higher. But God saw that they were trying to gain too much power. God changed their one language into many, so that their words sounded like babble to each other. The people had to stop building the tower, because they could no longer understand each other.

With a friend, try building a model of the Tower of Babel, together, without any talking. Which part was most difficult, and why?

_____

_____

_____

_____

_____

The Language of Our Past, Present, and Future

Having a common language unites us and brings Am Yisrael closer together. It is important to understanding much of our history and traditions, starting with the Torah, which is written in Hebrew.

Many of the prayers in our siddur, our prayer book, are written in Hebrew, too. So when Jews pray in one corner of the world, they are saying the same words as Jews in another corner of the world.

The Sh'ma is one of our oldest and most important prayers. Its words come from the Torah. Instead of being a prayer directed to God, the Sh'ma is a message for Am Yisrael.

שְׁמַע יִשְׂרָאֵל יְיָ אֱלֹהֵינוּ יְיָ אֶחָד.

Sh'ma Yisrael, Adonai Eloheinu, Adonai Echad.
Hear, O Israel! Adonai is our God, Adonai is One. (Deuteronomy 6:4)

Why do you think this prayer begins with the words "Hear, O Israel"?

_____

When you say the Sh'ma, what message are you sharing with other Jews?

_____

Words to Know: Mezuzah

A *mezuzah* is a small scroll made from parchment on which the Sh'ma is written. *Mezuzot* (more than one mezuzah) are usually placed in decorative cases and hung on the doorposts of Jewish houses and synagogues.

An Ancient Language Blooms Again

How did a little boy, a cat, and a dog help create the modern Hebrew language?

Today, millions of people in Israel and around the world speak Hebrew. It seems natural to us that the Jewish state would have chosen Hebrew as its official language. But in the 1800s, Hebrew wasn't a language for everyday use; it was the language in which the Torah was written and in which prayers were recited. So how did this ancient language become a part of modern life?

Eliezer Ben-Yehuda

"Dabeir Ivrit!" Eliezer Ben-Yehuda liked to tell his friends and family. "Speak Hebrew!" Ever since he was a little boy, Eliezer had been studying Hebrew. When he grew up and moved to Palestine (in 1881), as the Land of Israel was called then, he saw that Jews there came from many countries and spoke many different languages. He thought that if everyone would speak Hebrew, then they could understand each other. So he worked night and day to make Hebrew a spoken language once again.

kelev
כֶּלֶב

At home, Eliezer and his wife, Devorah, spoke only Hebrew to their son, Ben-Tzion, who became the first baby in more than a thousand years to be raised as a Hebrew speaker. It took three years until he said his first words, but his parents were happy to hear him finally say, *"Abba* [father]!"

Since their friends did not speak Hebrew, Eliezer brought home a cat and a dog on which his children could practice. They named the dog Maheir, the Hebrew word for "fast," hoping the dog would be true to his name and run quickly.

Eliezer and Devorah soon discovered that there were not enough words in Hebrew for everything their family wanted to say. Their children couldn't ask for ice cream or an omelet, a doll or a bicycle—there were no words in the Torah for these things! So Eliezer created new Hebrew words, and the Hebrew language grew along with his and Devorah's children.

Hebrew is now a thriving modern language in the State of Israel.

g'lidah
גְּלִידָה

Ben Yehuda Street, Jerusalem, Israel

Words Make a Difference

Did you know that there are only 8,000 Hebrew words in the Torah but over 120,000 modern Hebrew words? Eliezer Ben-Yehuda and his family spent years researching the Hebrew language, coming up with new words, and putting all this hard work together in the first Hebrew dictionary. In fact, Eliezer even coined the Hebrew word for dictionary, *milon*, from the Hebrew *milah*, which means "word."

Your Turn

How is your Hebrew? You probably know more than you realize. Think about the Hebrew words that you have learned in this class, from your family, or in your synagogue. Create a dictionary or scrapbook of the Hebrew words you know so that your friends can learn them too.

Talk about It

What other Hebrew words would you like to learn? How does the Hebrew language connect you with Jews around the world?

Hebrew Lessons

Learn some more Hebrew by filling in this crossword puzzle with the English meanings for each Hebrew word. Many of these Hebrew words come straight from the Bible. Others were created by Eliezer Ben-Yehuda.

Across:

2. בֻּבָּה *Bubah*, a toy that can be dressed up.

4. חַשְׁמַל *Ḥashmal*, what we use to power our lights and computers, based on the biblical word for something that glitters.

5. כּוֹס *Kos*, an object you drink from.

8. קֶשֶׁת *Keshet*, the sign God gave Noah to show the world would never be destroyed by a flood again.

9. אוֹפַנַּיִם *Ofanayim*, an object with wheels that's fun to ride.

10. צְפַרְדֵּעַ *Tz'fardei'a*, the second of the Ten Plagues; it kept the Egyptians hopping.

Down:

1. גְּלִידָה *G'lidah*, a frozen dessert.

2. חֲלוֹמוֹת *Halomot*, the thoughts we have while we sleep. The biblical character Joseph was famous for his.

3. אֲוִירוֹן *Aviron*, a modern invention that makes travel fast. The word comes from the Hebrew word *avir*, meaning "air."

6. קוֹל *Kol*, what we use to speak. The Israeli radio channel is called *Kol Yisrael* because it speaks for all of Israel.

7. גַּרְבַּיִם *Garbayim*, an item of clothing that keeps your feet warm, from the Arabic word *garub*.

CHAPTER 5

LEARNING BY DOING: SYMBOLS AND RITUALS

Take a close look at the flag of Israel, the Jewish state. What Jewish symbol do you see in the middle? What other Jewish symbols can you name? Symbols and rituals connect us to the Jewish community in many ways.

How the Flag Got Its Star and Stripes

You may be familiar with the six-pointed Star of David, or *Magen David*, in the center of Israel's flag. Did you also know that the stripes on the flag were designed to look like the stripes of a *tallit*, a Jewish prayer shawl? The design of this flag uses symbols to reflect the fact that Israel is a Jewish country. Today, the flag is used proudly in Israel as well as in synagogues and Jewish schools across the globe. The flag itself is a modern Jewish symbol based on a traditional Jewish object.

Identifying Jewish Symbols

Like the Jewish star and the Israeli flag, symbols are designs or objects that remind us of something important in our culture. Symbols unite us through the language of our senses, whether it's the sight of a beautiful silver ornament crowning a Torah scroll, the awe-inspiring sound of the shofar, or the taste of a crisp matzah at the seder.

Can you identify each of these Jewish symbols? Where else have you seen them?

What does each of them represent to you?

In Good Taste

Sweet ḥaroset or fresh crispy latkes—these delicious items enhance our Jewish holidays and mean so much more. Many traditional holiday foods are symbols that remind us of our past or represent hopes for the future. So the apples we dip in honey on Rosh Hashanah not only taste good, but also are a good-luck symbol as we hope for a "good and sweet year."

Can you identify the holiday foods shown up close here?

On which holidays do we eat them, and why?

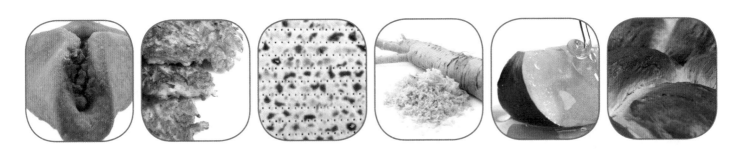

A Hands-On Tradition

How do you feel when you light the Ḥanukkah menorah each year? What is it like to eat matzah at a Passover seder? Our Jewish tradition is full of activities that help us fully experience holidays or other special events. We call these activities rituals. Having the same rituals in common with other members of the Jewish community unites us and gives us ways to celebrate and observe together.

Holiday-Style

Physical objects, like a seder plate or a shofar, help us make rituals more meaningful. See how many ritual objects you recognize by solving the riddles on the next page.

Word Bank:

shofar

gragger

Kiddush cup

Ḥanukkah menorah

candlesticks

dreidel

seder plate

Holiday Word Bank:
Shabbat
Rosh Hashanah
Yom Kippur
Ḥanukkah
Purim
Passover

What Am I?

I am a...   **My holiday or holidays**

1. Light me for eight nights to recall the miracle of the oil and the victory of the Maccabees.

2. My light welcomes in a restful holiday every week.

3. Use me to drown out the name of the evil villain Haman.

4. I hold a roasted shank bone, ḥaroset, and other symbolic foods that help us remember the Exodus from Egypt.

5. Spin and win! My letters stand for *Nes gadol hayah sham*, "A great miracle happened there."

6. Fill me with wine or grape juice and recite a special blessing.

7. *Teki'ah*. . . . I make a bold sound that will get your attention.

Meet Joseph

Joseph celebrates Jewish holidays with an Italian twist, with family members in different Jewish communities across Italy.

Favorite Jewish Holiday: Rosh Hashanah. Italian Jews have two Rosh Hashanah seders, where we eat foods that are symbols of good luck for the New Year. First we make Kiddush. For each food, we say a special blessing. My grandfather writes *Shanah Tovah* (Happy New Year) in Hebrew on the tablecloth using grains of wheat. After the second night, these seeds are placed on saucers, on top of wet cotton pads, where they sprout and grow leaves. We use the seedlings to decorate the sukkah table two weeks later.

Favorite Food: *Bollo!* It's not only my favorite Jewish food, it's my favorite food period. Bollo is a sweet plum cake with lots of raisins, very fluffy, that is brushed with egg yolk and sugar before baking to make it crunchy on top. We eat it at the end of Yom Kippur, when we break the fast.

Shabbat in the Community

No matter what day, month, or season it is, we have a holiday to look forward to this week—Shabbat. As with the other Jewish holidays, there are rituals and symbols to help make Shabbat a day like no other. We remember the ancient Israelites' promise to celebrate Shabbat each time we welcome it with beautiful songs and with ritual blessings over candles, wine, and ḥallah. While the Shabbat lights twinkle, we treat Shabbat like a royal guest, with a fine meal at a table set with the best china.

In the synagogue, we welcome Shabbat on Friday evenings with prayers and melodies created just for Shabbat. On Saturday mornings, the Torah is the star of the Shabbat service. A portion of the Bible is read each week before the whole congregation. Did you know that the same portion is read on the same day in every synagogue around the world?

A Tree of Life

A number of rituals accompany the Torah reading to show how important the Torah is to us. The scroll itself is dressed in fine fabrics and gold and silver objects. As the Torah is carried from or returned to the Ark where it is kept, the congregation sings. One song compares the Torah to a tree, saying, "It is a tree of life to those who hold it fast" (Proverbs 3:18).

Trees give us fruit and shade. On each branch, fill in something the Torah gives us.

Trees need water, earth, and sunlight. On each root, write something the Torah needs from us, as part of our Brit, our covenant with God to pass down the Torah to Am Yisrael now and in the future.

Torah

The Art of the Ritual

After our ancestors received the Ten Commandments at Mount Sinai, they built a beautiful Ark for the tablets and housed them in an exquisite portable temple called the *Mishkan*, or Tabernacle, which they carried through the Sinai desert to the Land of Israel. Every object in the Mishkan was carefully crafted from the best materials—the seven-branched menorah was forged from pure gold, and the Holy Ark was made of beautiful wood covered in gold. Ever since then, Jews have practiced *hidur mitzvah*, making our celebrations more extraordinary and more meaningful by using beautiful ritual objects. Our Jewish sages said:

Ceremonial cup, Breslau, 1752

Make a beautiful sukkah in God's honor, a beautiful lulav, a beautiful shofar, beautiful tzitzit, and a beautiful Scroll of the Law [Torah], and write it with fine ink, a fine reed [pen], and a skilled scribe, and wrap it with beautiful silks. (Talmud, Shabbat 133b)

In every country where Jews have lived, Jewish artists have put their own unique stamp on traditional objects, using local materials and styles. The result is a dazzling array of ceremonial objects from communities far and wide.

Your Turn

Create your own design for a Jewish ceremonial item. First make a plan:

1. What object will you design? _____

   _____

2. How will it be used? _____

   _____

3. What materials will you use? _____

   _____

4. What Hebrew words, Jewish symbols, or other decorations will you add to it? _____

   _____

Talk about It

How do our holiday celebrations at home or in the synagogue link us to Jews around the world? In what ways do our ritual objects make our celebrations more meaningful?

Now draw a sketch of your design here. Then gather your materials and start creating!

CHAPTER 6

BECOMING OUR BEST SELVES: Mitzvot

Think about your typical day. What do you do to help yourself have the best day possible? You might eat an apple because it gives you energy or set the table to help with dinner. The Torah also gives us things to do to improve our lives—they're called *mitzvot*.

Mitzvot Build Community

The Torah guides each of us to become a better person every day. To help us, it provides a pathway of proper behaviors, called *mitzvot*. There are many kinds of mitzvot, such as celebrating Shabbat or not lying. We share these mitzvot, and our Jewish values, with the Jewish community around the world. Our sages taught:

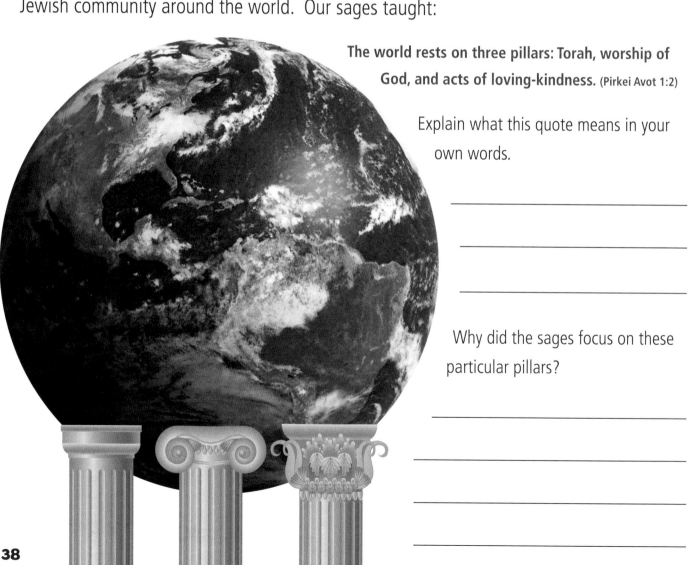

The world rests on three pillars: Torah, worship of God, and acts of loving-kindness. (Pirkei Avot 1:2)

Explain what this quote means in your own words.

_____

_____

_____

Why did the sages focus on these particular pillars?

_____

_____

_____

_____

Words to Know: Mitzvah

The word *mitzvah* means "commandment," an action described in the Torah for all Jews to do. More than one mitzvah are called *mitzvot*.

All Kinds of Mitzvot

Did you know that there are 613 mitzvot in the Torah? They can be divided into two categories: mitzvot that guide us in how we treat other people; and mitzvot that guide us in our relationship with God, such as through ritual observances like putting up a mezuzah or having a Passover seder.

Think about the mitzvot listed below. Which category do you think they fall into? Check the appropriate box and then explain why each mitzvah is important. Why do you think we need both kinds of mitzvot?

	Mitzvah between people	Mitzvah between us and God	This mitzvah is important because…
Saying the Sh'ma			
Not stealing			
Hearing the shofar			
Not embarrassing others			
Giving tzedakah			
Eating in a sukkah			
Celebrating Shabbat			
Honoring one's parents			

The Importance of Caring

The Torah gives us many mitzvot to show us how to be fair and kind to other people. The underlying rule is found in the Torah: "Love your neighbor as yourself" (Leviticus 19:18).

Why do you think the Torah tells us to care about other people as much as we care about ourselves?

_____

_____

What are some ways we can be fair and kind to others?

_____

_____

Welcoming Guests

Famous for his kindness, our ancestor Abraham set the standard for all of Am Yisrael. His giving began at home. According to Jewish legend, his tent was open on all sides as a sign to travelers that they were welcome to enter freely, to rest and to eat. Our sages tell us that Abraham even planted an orchard so that he could offer his guests the sweet fruit. Abraham included everyone in his household in the mitzvah of *hachnasat orḥim*, welcoming guests, by teaching them to care for others as he did.

Describe a time when someone went out of his or her way to welcome you. _____

_____

_____

How did it make you feel?_____

_____

Torah on the Go

Which mitzvah best teaches us how to handle each situation below? Write the letter of the mitzvah on the line. There might be more than one choice for some situations.

Which mitzvah can help you in each of these situations?

_____ **1.** You find a wallet on the sidewalk.

_____ **2.** Your classmate who tripped you yesterday walks past your desk.

_____ **3.** Your friend looks funny because she is wearing mismatched socks.

_____ **4.** You see a game in a store that you really want, but you don't have money to buy it.

_____ **5.** A customer forgets to take his or her change at your lemonade stand.

_____ **6.** The swing in your backyard is loose.

_____ **7.** Your sister asks you if she should lie to your mother about having finished her homework.

_____ **8.** You are still upset with your friend because she didn't invite you to a party last month.

_____ **9.** You worked on a project with a classmate and want to complain to your best friend that he did a bad job.

_____ **10.** You have been saving to buy a new video game, but then someone asks you to donate some money to a children's hospital.

Mitzvah Bank

a. Do not steal.

b. Make sure there is nothing dangerous in your home.

c. Give charity.

d. Return lost property to its owner.

e. Don't speak badly of other people.

f. Deal fairly in business.

g. Don't give bad advice.

h. Don't take revenge.

i. Don't embarrass others.

j. Don't hold a grudge.

Decide which three mitzvot you think are the most important and draw a ✡ next to each one. Then name another rule that you think should be added to this list and explain why it is important.

_____

_____

Fixing the World

Tikun olam, which means "repairing the world" in Hebrew, is the Jewish value of improving conditions for others, such as helping people in need or taking care of the environment. What do you think is "broken" in the world, and how can you help fix it?

Did you know that the State of Israel sent teams of experts to Haiti to help after the earthquake in 2010? Or that many Jews in America sent aid to Japan after the 2011 earthquake and tsunami? Judaism teaches us to help out around the world as well as in our own community. Jews throughout the ages have also helped other Jewish communities in danger, guided by the teaching, "All Israel is responsible for one another" (Talmud, Sh'vuot 39a).

Your Tikun Olam Personality

There are many ways to help fix the world. Some people look out for everyone they meet, some prefer to take care of our natural world, some work to build the Jewish community, and others speak out for justice. What is your tikun olam personality? Take the quiz on the next page to find out.

Your Turn

Be a "light for all nations," the prophet Isaiah instructed us (Isaiah 49:6). As Jews, we believe this means leading the way in making the world a better place. With your friends or classmates, make a list of tikun olam projects you would like to do. Vote on your favorite one. Whose help would you need? What would you need to do first? Next?

What's Your Way of Changing the World?

1. Which one of the following biblical stories inspires you the most?

    a. Moses and his brother Aaron confronting Pharoah and fighting for the Israelites' freedom.

    b. Rebecca giving water to a foreign traveler and his camels.

    c. Noah saving the animals by taking them onto the ark and caring for them during the flood.

    d. Mordechai and Esther saving Am Yisrael from destruction at the hands of Haman, in Persia.

2. Jewish leaders inspire their followers with their messages. Whose words do you like best?

    a. The prophet Amos taught, "Hate evil and love good, and establish justice at the gate [of the city] . . ." (Amos 5:15).

    b. The sage Hillel advised, "Be a student . . . loving and pursuing peace, loving all people, and bringing them closer to Torah" (Pirkei Avot 1:12).

    c. Ruth W. Messinger, the president of the American Jewish World Service, says, "I feel a deep responsibility to assist those in the world who are . . . living in abject poverty."

    d. Theodore Herzl, who worked to establish the modern State of Israel, wrote, "If you will [wish for] it, it is no dream."

3. You want to volunteer in your synagogue. Which of the following would you choose?

    a. Write a story about a problem in the world for your synagogue's newsletter.

    b. Help out in the kindergarten class in your religious school.

    c. Collect gently used clothing to donate to a homeless shelter.

    d. Raise money for a Jewish community in need.

4. Which of the following community-related activities would you do first?

    a. Help a friend run an election campaign for class president at school.

    b. Volunteer at a soup kitchen that makes nutritious meals for needy families.

    c. Join an environmental group that cleans parks and plants trees.

    d. Help plan the Ḥanukkah party at your religious school.

If you answered . . .

Mostly a's: You are a **seeker of justice**—you like to make sure that laws are fair and that justice prevails.

Mostly b's: You are a **believer in kindness**—you care about every individual and give generously of your time.

Mostly c's: You are a **caretaker of the world**—you are concerned with the survival of people around the world and the environment.

Mostly d's: You are a **builder of a nation**—you are always thinking about the future of Am Yisrael and do your best to build both the Jewish nation and the Land of Israel.

Does this sound like you? How would you describe your tikun olam personality in your own words? _____

_____

_____

_____

_____

Tzedakah as a way of life

One way we can help improve the world is by contributing money or other resources such as food, clothing, or even our time and effort. The mitzvah of giving to those in need is called **tzedakah**.

Giving tzedakah is an important part of Jewish life. We are taught to look out for the poor in our own community and in other communities around the world. We can make it a regular habit to give tzedakah, by putting money in a tzedakah box every week before Shabbat or before Jewish holidays.

Words to Know: Tzedek

The word *tzedakah* comes from the Hebrew word ***tzedek***, which means "justice" or "being fair." Tzedakah is not the same as charity, because giving tzedakah is an obligation, something we must do whether we want to or not.

DONATION BOX

Meet Jack

For his bar mitzvah project, Jack raised more than $3,000 to buy mosquito nets to prevent Jewish children in Ethiopia from catching malaria carried by mosquitoes.

How I Found a Cause: For her bat mitzvah, my older sister collected school supplies for Ethiopian kids in Israel. I chose to do mosquito nets because of how big a deal malaria is in Ethiopia. With these nets, we can help protect families from a potentially fatal disease.

How My Mitzvah Project Worked: My mom and I talked to the North American Conference on Ethiopian Jewry about setting up a fund-raising web page. We sent the link to members of our synagogue and all of our friends. We also included a note in my bar mitzvah invitation asking people to donate, and we put out information about the project in our temple, along with a can for donations.

What I Learned: How easy it is to make a big difference in people's lives. I learned how amazing it is that just by sending one net to Ethiopia, we saved somebody's life.

Taking It to the Highest Level

The Torah teaches that it is not enough just to give. The mitzvah of tzedakah is described in this way:

> **If there is a needy person among you…do not harden your heart, and do not shut your hand from your needy brother.…Give to him readily and have no regrets.** (Deuteronomy 15:7–8, 15:10)

What do you think it means to "give readily and have no regrets"?

_____

The Jewish philosopher Maimonides described eight levels of giving tzedakah:

1. Giving a loan or helping somebody find a job so he or she will no longer need tzedakah.

2. Giving anonymously: neither giver nor recipient knows each other.

3. Giver knows recipient; recipient does not know giver.

4. Recipient knows giver; giver does not know recipient.

5. Giving before being asked.

6. Giving generously after being asked.

7. Giving willingly, but not a lot.

8. Giving unwillingly.

Talk about It

Think about a time when you personally helped somebody in need. How did it make you feel? How do mitzvot connect us to others in our community?

Choose two levels from the tzedakah ladder. How could you give tzedakah in a way that fits each of those levels? _____

_____

What are some similarities or differences about giving in each of these two ways?

_____

_____

CHAPTER 7

YOUR JEWISH IDENTITY

What have you learned about being Jewish from people in your family or community? Which Jewish experiences mean the most to you?

Part of a Community

Being part of Am Yisrael means that you are part of a community with a shared history, stories, language, symbols, traditions, and values that will guide you at every stage of your life. As you grow, your Jewish identity will influence all that you do.

Your Turn

Now it's your turn to share what you like about being Jewish and being a part of Am Yisrael. Work with a partner and interview each other. You can make up your own questions or use the ones on the facing page. Write up your interview, or record it for the class.

Meet _____

Who is your favorite Jewish hero from the Torah or other Jewish stories? Why?

_____

What do you think are two of the most important mitzvot? Why are they so important?

_____

Do you have relatives who live in other Jewish communities in North America or across the world? Where?

_____

Describe how you and your family celebrate your favorite Jewish holiday.

_____

What questions do you still have about being Jewish? What things would you like to learn more about?

_____

Checklist

Give yourself a big check mark for each of the **Your Turn** experiences you have tried.

- [ ] Taste different types of ḥaroset, page 13
- [ ] Interview a parent or grandparent about your family history, page 19
- [ ] Make a dictionary or scrapbook of Hebrew words, page 28
- [ ] Design a Jewish ceremonial object, page 37
- [ ] Plan a tikun olam project, page 42
- [ ] Interview a classmate about his or her Jewish identity, pages 46–47

What other Jewish experiences have you tried for the first time this year?

✔ _____

✔ _____

✔ _____

WORDS TO KNOW

Am Yisrael Hebrew for "the people of Israel;" the worldwide Jewish community.

Brit Hebrew for "covenant" or "agreement;" the agreement made between God and Abraham, renewed by the Jewish people and Moses at Mt. Sinai, to honor the Torah and pass it down to future generations.

Diaspora The Jewish communities around the word, living outside of Israel.

Israelites The Jewish people in ancient times; the descendents of Jacob, who was also known as Israel.

Kotel Also called the Western Wall, the remains of the ancient Temple complex in Jerusalem; the holiest site for the Jewish people.

Mezuzah A small scroll placed in a decorative case and usually hung on the doorposts of Jewish houses and synagogues.

Mitzvah Hebrew for "commandment;" an action described in the Torah for all Jews to do (plural: *mitzvot*).

Temple The center for Jewish worship in ancient Israel. The First Temple, also known as Solomon's Temple, was replaced by the Second Temple, which stood until the year 70 CE.

Tikun Olam Hebrew for "repairing the world;" the mitzvah of improving conditions in the world, such as by helping people in need or caring for the environment.

Torah Also called the Five Books of Moses; the first part of the Bible, which contains our most important stories and laws.

19th century tzedakah box, Charleston, South Carolina

Tzedakah From the Hebrew word *tzedek*, which means "justice" or "being fair;" the mitzvah of giving to those in need.